KEEP THE **FIRE** OF **GOD'S WORD BURNING** IN YOUR **HEART**

LET THE LIGHT OF GOD'S WORD BURN

Gerald Scott Melton

Author's Tranquility Press
ATLANTA, GEORGIA

Gerald Scott Melton/Author's Tranquility Press
3900 N Commerce Dr. Suite 300 #1255
Atlanta, GA 30344, USA
www.authorstranquilitypress.com

Ordering Information:
Quantity sales. Special discounts are available on quantity purchases by corporations, associations, and others. For details, contact the "Special Sales Department" at the address above.

Keep the Fire of God's Word Buring in your Heart / Gerald Scott Melton

Paperback: 978-1-964037-23-3

eBook: 978-1-964037-24-0

Contents

Introduction

Do you know that it is up to you to keep the fire of biblical influence burning in your life? But why must you keep such fire in your heart? We find that the light of biblical influence appears only to be a trickle of what it used to be at the beginning of the current history of this nation (Christopher Columbus on). I believe that bible influence has less impact on the American people than it used to. It is my conclusion that biblical influence keeps us out of dark spirituality. Therefore, keeping the bible's influence in our lives is pertinent for godly living. I am writing this book to help us from falling into a trap of allowing biblical influence to go out of our life.

Do not permit biblical influence to go out of your life. Why should we keep such influence? Here are a few good reasons:

Biblical influence is vitally necessary for God's light to shine on your life, it is basic living content for your life, and God's Word is to be the authoritative rule for life (a basic defense for you).

Biblical influence is vital also if we will retain the biblical way of life.

Biblical influence is vital for God's persuasion for living.

Biblical influence is vital because the godly process continues operating when we observe its contents and practice it.

<u>Let's break down the idea of my thesis:</u>
<u>1. It is essential, 2. We refuse to allow, 3. Biblical influence, 4. To go out of our lives.</u>

1. **It is essential means:**

a) Anything indispensable. CED dictionary

b) Absolutely and vitally necessary. CED dictionary

c) Basic and fundamental.

d) Required.

2. **Refuse to allow means:**

a) Make no concession for allowing.

b) Concede, not to allow.

3. **Biblical influence means:**

a) Scripture persuasion.

b) The Westminster Dictionary of Theological Terms. Donald K. McKim. Pg 29, "Bible, authority of the: Recognition of the bible status and function as providing a source and norm for such elements as belief, conduct, and the experience of God."

c) Scripture gives saving knowledge as to God's salvation and proper worship, and reveals God's glory.

4. **To go out of our lives means:**

a) To depart from us.

b) To leave us.

c) A light going out.

d) To have no influence of it on us.

e) To have removal of it from us.

<u>I WANT MY INTRODUCTION TO SHOW US THAT WE DON'T HAVE TO ALLOW BIBLICAL INFLUENCE TO GO OUT OF OUR LIVES.</u>

Americans have a unique situation. We have become cut-off and aloof from our biblical settings and roots. With the removal of the bible and prayer out of school and the systematic removal of God out of society; we opened the door to all kinds of evils, crime, drugs, warfare, etc. This is constantly allowed by the government to force a progressive secular humanistic society. This style of oppression is nationwide, and all America is affected.

With the gates of hell operating in companies, organizations, governments, and within people's hearts; it is no-wonder the nation is getting lost further day by day. Many have taken the means of championing the cause to struggle to keep awareness of God and the utter need for his Word to be open to the American people. Who is going to help us face this lack of devotees to God's powerful Word. We have to practice and demand the right within society and in our personal lives to respect and study scripture.

We must find and work with like precious persons within our communities that share a passion for Jesus. These have to be people committed to the study of the Word of God. 2 Timothy 3:10-17, tells us the Word is our tool in life for everything. Here is an Acronym that we should keep in our mind:

a) B: basic
b) I: instructions
c) B: before
d) L: leaving
e) E: earth

The bible is to be known and studied.

We must maintain the right and freedom to read and comment on scriptures. Prayer must now be our over-arching guard. The very next step is learning to read and study the Word of God for its daily applications for life. Our goal is to plot our schedule for the journey of what study we will do and when.

Personal Analysis 1

If we keep biblical influence burning in our heart, we will have to analyze our life. I suggest we start with where we want to go as a disciple of Jesus Christ, and observe how God's Word can take us there by the help of the Holy Spirit.

We have to begin by asking, "Who am I?" Where am I in the spiritual contextual setting of being Jesus's disciple in walk, deeds, spiritual disciplines, and commitment. We need to allow Scripture to speak to these areas of who and where I am in relationship with Jesus.

Going on, we ask, "Am I a disciple of Jesus Christ yet?" Have I committed to him? Will I follow him no-matter how bad or good it gets? How does or doesn't my life demonstrate I follow and pursue Jesus Christ? Let your knowledge of scripture address these things.

Am I currently following Jesus yet? Am I born again? This simply means you decided to turn to God through faith in Jesus Christ, and did this through a prayer of petitioning God for help through Jesus. Acknowledging your need for Jesus and his atoning sacrifice on your behalf and his eternal life imputed into your heart. Next, you want to study the scriptures so that you can grow in God. You also want to be able to study, so you can articulate your faith. Does your faith persuade you to serve God and others, so you have a pleasing account for God when you enter eternity and give account? You will want to learn to study scripture in a good way where you draw necessary nourishment daily. What system do you use? A very basic plan is to study 1 to 3 chapters a day, using a dictionary to look up the words.

We want to ask, "As I study scripture, what principles am I learning that will help my leadership in life?" What Christian community should I join to facilitate God's will in my life? What interactions with others demonstrate I am growing in biblical leadership? How faithful is my leadership?

What does the bible say about stewardship? Have I surrendered all aspects of my life to the plan of God over me? How does the bible tell me to steward each area of my life? What is my purpose in life? You will have to search this out. What are the consequences of being faithful or unfaithful to God?

Am I willing to fight for this way of life? Will I seek God if I get tired and want to quit; so that God can give me strength to go on? How do I learn to fight the right enemy? What does the bible tell us about spiritual warfare? How important is spiritual warfare if I will continue in biblical influence? Where does prayer fit in with this?

As you read the bible, let God stir up answers to your questions. If you have questions, ask God for the answers as you read the bible. Your answers may not be what others are, necessarily. As you study and stay close to God, you can be assured that he will express his will to you in some way. Perhaps scripture will come to your mind, a godly idea will emerge, or perhaps God will speak to you? As you pray, God will communicate to you in some way what his will is.

Personal Analysis 2

Keep the light of God's Word, or refusing to allow biblical influence to go out of our lives.

We have to plan for this: To rekindle the fire for God's Word, fan it into flame, and overcome evil with good.

We have to set goals: Work out our study plan, put it into practice, and translate the application into communication to God by prayer.

Of these things put them in remembrance, charging them before the Lord that they strive not about words to no profit, but to the subverting of the hearers. Study to shew thyself approved unto God, a workman that needeth not to be ashamed, rightly dividing the word of truth. 2 Timothy 2:14-15 (KJV)

But continue thou in the things which thou hast learned and hast been assured of, knowing of whom thou hast learned them; And that from a child thou hast known the holy scriptures, which can make thee wise unto salvation through faith which is in Christ Jesus. All scripture is given by inspiration of God, and is profitable for doctrine, for reproof, for correction, for instruction in righteousness: That the man of God may be perfect, thoroughly furnished unto all good works. 2 Timothy 3:14-17 (KJV)

And the things that thou hast heard of me among many witnesses, the same commit thou to faithful men, who shall be able to teach others as well. 2 Timothy 2:2 (KJV)

Therefore, I endure all things for the elect's sake, that they may also obtain the salvation which is in Christ Jesus with eternal glory. 2 Timothy 2:10 (KJV)

Our responsibilities should be to:

Learn, know, and apply scripture.

Know doctrine (bible teaching).

Know how to study, observe, interpret, and apply scripture.

Trust God, his Word, and his promises.

Hold the biblical scripture as our rule of life.

Personal Analysis–3

Apply yourself to the study of the Word of God.

What will be your focus for today as you study? Daily, to achieve one's personal goals, we must begin with a plan. Once we got our objectives in place, and we know how we want our study to go, put the goal into motion: work the daily study plan out and put it into practice while translating it into communication with God by prayer.

What is the object of attention? We will attend to where we put focus daily. Today, what focus will our study center on? What topic? What passage? Once that is known, then ask the who, what, when, where, why, and how about it. Do a personal study on the passage. Ask, why am I doing this study? What happens if I don't do this or disobey? How can I apply it?

What will I need to do this study? There will be the need for time, resources to facilitate learning, a good attitude, great study habits, attention and focus. Stay focused on your goals and objectives, and finally, ask great study questions.

You will stir up the flame with the fuel of God as needed. Ask God to guide your study. Ask God to take you into his treasure house of good's. Have faith in God's Word. Pray over the study.

Recall the passion which God has stirred in your being. As you experience the presence of God, write how he stirs you on paper. Write down your findings and applications on paper. How did the Word move you? What life application will you make?

How is the grace applied to the object of attention? How do the results demand

God's help and grace. How do the results demand our dependence on God?

The aspects of purpose needed are what? How does this study call your spiritual trade into action?

Personal Analysis-4

We must ask ourselves questions to understand how and where we want to go.

Who am I? What is the testimony I bear? To what has God called me to do? What are my inner values which I won't violate? We follow Jesus Christ by respecting the Word of God as the authoritative rule for life. We get to the Father through Jesus, and we get to Jesus through scripture. We do this to love and serve God and fellowship with him. The goal is to read, comment, and use scripture for all of life's needs.

Can you describe where you came from, did you learn anything from that? Many of us have been cut off and estranged from God's Word. We learned that learning to know about God and develop a living walk with him is what life is about. All our days are to be lived pleasing God.

What about right now, do you still struggle? We may be struggling and yet aware of our need for God and his Word. Hopefully, now, or in a little bit, you will be pursuing God through scripture.

If I stay on the course, and I'm on with God, what will the future hold for me if things remain the same? I will tell you: If you don't make the necessary changes, it's likely that nothing will change? If ignorance is our constant friend, then we will be most miserable. If we pursue God and find him, then we will be blessed if we pursue with hot interest.

What then is it we are pursuing for our future with God leading our lives? Is our vision full of God, blessings, hope, and divine order. If we can see such a vision; let's establish the means to acquire the knowledge and experiential walk with God that will last forever.

What are the resources we need to get to the walk and relationship with God we so desire? We obviously need the Word, good study habits, and discipline.

What is in our way of achieving this walk with God? Are the gates of hell pressing, do we lack prayer, is there the smell of spiritual warfare, fear, failure to start our journey? We are to use scripture to address our relationships. Are we failing to plan for our fellowship with God? No resources, or applications? No seeking and clinging to God?

These are just some questions we have to answer to begin to formulate an idea of the types of things God is addressing in scripture.

Personal Analysis–5

In the conclusion of our analysis to refuse to allow biblical influence to go out of our lives, let's analyze how to do so.

Chaos and estrangement for Christian's fervency for God's Word is directly coming against the believer by the gates of hell. The enemy is attempting to seize the objectives of confrontation at every community event he thinks he can win. So as God and the Word are systematically removed out of societies; they, in turn, are systematically turned into hell. This removal of God is now allowed by our courts, governments, our people, our organizations, schools, and every place we have gatherings.

Hell, angry people, and many other groups would attempt to seize our journey by misusing scripture to do so. This is typical of God's Word in Church history. We learn in all of this that maintaining the Word requires our cross and our blood. Satan, through Church compromise, enlightenment, and irrational and bogus attacks by various movements, are again attempting to put out the fire of God's Word. The least amount of damage they try to do is put the fire from men's hearts.

Satan wants to steal the Word out of a man's heart as soon as it is put there. We must remain vigilant.

When anyone hears the word of the kingdom, and understands it not, then cometh the wicked one, and catcheth away that which was sown in his heart. This is he which received seed by the wayside. Matthew 13:19 (KJV)

Guard the good deposit and your heart affections with all diligence. The Word is pertinent to a clean conscience, but biblical reading must be maintained. We hold a theology of God's Word. We either keep it and are kept by it, or we reject it and are rejected.

I charge thee therefore before God, and the Lord Jesus Christ, who shall judge the quick and the dead at his appearing and his kingdom; Preach the word; be instant in season, out of season; reprove, rebuke, exhort with all long suffering and doctrine. For the time will come when they will not endure sound doctrine; but after their own lusts shall they heap to themselves teachers, having itching ears; And they shall turn away their ears from the truth, and shall be turned unto fables. 2 Timothy 4:1-4 (KJV)

These verses express immediate and daily use of scripture to keep ourselves on course. In daily life, praying out our scripture studies is pertinent to the application of the study. As we pray, God aligns us up with his will. Seek God on how you can apply what you have learned. Seek God, also, as to how to use your study to deal with life's situations.

The light of God's Word

We can know the holy scriptures, which can make us wise unto salvation in Jesus Christ.

But thou hast fully known my doctrine, manner of life, purpose, faith, long suffering, charity, patience, persecutions, afflictions, which came unto me at Antioch, at Iconium, at Lystra; what persecutions I endured: but out of them all the Lord delivered me. Yea, and all that will live godly in Christ Jesus shall suffer persecution. But evil men and seducers shall wax worse and worse, deceiving, and being deceived. But continue thou in the things which thou hast learned and hast been assured of, knowing of whom thou hast learned them; and that from a child thou hast known the holy scriptures, which are able to make thee wise unto salvation through faith which is in Christ Jesus. All scripture is given by inspiration of God, and is profitable for doctrine, for reproof, for correction, for instruction in righteousness: That the man of God may be perfect, thoroughly furnished unto all good works. 2 Timothy 3:10-17 (KJV)

I want to show four ideas that I derived from the above passage, which will help us see how God's holy Word will make us wise unto salvation.

First, God's holy Word will make us wise unto salvation by giving us direction through our persecutions and troubles by God's help.

As we learn scripture, our purpose becomes defined, our battles emerge, and God's salvation delivers us. The passage tells us, "Thou haste fully known my doctrine." We need to know our bible, so we can endure our persecutions.

Only as we learn, live, and retain the walk with God by scripture, we can overcome. Victory is not destroying your competition, but starting the day with God and ending with him in unbroken fellowship.

The bible is our greatest tool which the Holy Spirit uses to encourage us in God's divine will as we grow, live and war a good warfare.

Second, God's holy Word will make us wise unto salvation through the backlash that comes to those who live godly.

If we are followers of Christ, scripture instructs us to expect persecution. Scripture tells us "All that live godly…" As we follow Jesus, we are empowered to live godly. We learn from the passage that evil men will wax worse and worse. The future will be both full of good and evil.

So, how can our light shine amidst the darkness of such people. God shall be our light and his Word our lamp. God has not left us out there. We can know God and his will through the bible testimony.

Let us prepare for our warfare. Get the facts from scripture. No-matter what method we use to read scripture, read it to prepare thyself.

Third, God's holy Word will make us wise unto salvation as we continue in scripture training.

We are exhorted to continue in scripture training, so we know the bible, and we become wise in salvation which is in Jesus Christ. "Continue thou in the things…thou…hast been assured of." We are to stay in the truth to repel error.

Herein is hope for us all. Any man or woman can obtain God's salvation by faith in Jesus, as noted in the scriptures. Do you know you can get a job working for a company, if you qualify, apply, and are accepted? God offers salvation to you because you have sinned. All you have to do is ask and from there God will offer you satisfying work for him.

So, learn scripture, get in the book. Let God give you ideas freely. Follow through on those commands and ideas. You can expect after giving yourself to God that in time he will speak to you. Apply what God tells you and be on your way.

Fourth, God's holy Word will make us wise unto salvation because God gave the scriptures to inspire, direct, and instruct us unto every perfect work.

Scripture, as we see and understand, as we read, becomes the means God uses to perfect us for every good work. For, "all scripture is given by inspiration of God." As we read, God breathes into our soul. "That the man of God maybe perfect." God is bringing those who diligently follow his instruction to perfection.

We have every bit of godly instruction to do what God calls us to. Our key is to understand what we are dealing with and how scripture addresses it and us as we deal with it. Spiritual direction is our key to sustained growth, and it is God's way to address us to conform to Jesus Christ.

We, in scripture, have all we need to grow. We have to grow so we submit to God. Stay in scripture to be a person of God for the hour.

We must learn that holy scripture can make us wise unto salvation in Jesus Christ.

We cannot, sometimes, change the central settings of life. But we can focus on our obedience to God and his Word. Things do happen, but it's our responding biblically that pleases God and brings his desperately needed help. We can usually find scripture which directly or indirectly addresses the situation. As we apply the bible, if effects larger community in a profound way.

Society, now, tends to backlash against confessing believers. Since God gave the scriptures to inspire us, this helps us cut through the backlash of that which comes to the faithful. Let's read and stand for this reason: that as we check out our lives before scripture, God gives us purpose for life and victory as we continue to study.

If we make headway in God's will for our lives, we must come to grips with God's Word for our wellbeing. We are admonished to continue in these things within the written word. If I haven't done my preparations, then I am vulnerable and a voluntary victim. As we know holy scripture, we are made wise unto salvation through faith in Jesus Christ.

As we study, pray it out. Ask God to do his will over everything; expecting God to work with you through it. After the study, ask God to help you apply it and bless the study. Seek God's continued help, so you can deal with life's scenarios.

Chapter 1
The light of God's Word in men's hearts

The light of God's Word goes out of a complacent, wicked, and wayward heart because of a person's choices of darkness over light.

And this is the condemnation, that light is come into the world, and men loved darkness rather than light because their deeds were evil. For every one that doeth evil hateth the light, neither cometh to the light, lest his deeds should be reproved. But he that doeth truth cometh to the light, that his deeds may be made manifest, that they are wrought in God. John 3:19-21 (KJV)

Each individual has a choice to either like the light in Jesus Christ, or follow Satan (the darkness).

The light of God's Word goes out of a complacent, wicked, and wayward heart because a person is enticed to satisfy the flesh over the Spirit instead of following the Word which points to Christ.

For we know that the law is spiritual: but I am carnal, sold under sin. For that which I do I allow not: for what I would, that do I not, but what I hate that do I. If then I do that which I would not, I consent unto the law that it is good. Now then it is no more I that do it, but sin that dwelleth in me. For I know that in me (that is, in my flesh), dwelleth no good thing: for to will is present with me; but how to perform that which is good I find not. For the good that I would, I do not: but the evil which I would not, that I do? Now if I do that I would not, it is no more I that do it, but sin that dwelleth in me. Romans 7:14-20 (KJV)

We all have the right in choices to choose the Spirit or allow flesh to rule.

The light of God's Word goes out of a complacent, wicked, and wayward heart because a person abandons God and his plan.

Then Paul and Barnabas waxed bold, and said, it was necessary that the word of God should first have been spoken to you: but seeing ye put it from you, and judge yourselves unworthy of everlasting life, lo, we turn to the Gentiles. For so hath the Lord commanded us, saying, I have set thee to be a light of the Gentiles, that thou shouldest be for salvation unto the ends of the earth. Acts 13:46-47 (KJV)

To abandon God, his Word, and plan leads to corruption and idolatry; ultimately the second death.

The light of God's Word goes out of a complacent, wicked, and wayward heart because individuals allow their hearts to be carried away from truth by song, wine, woman, and materialism.

Heaven and earth shall pass away: but my words shall not pass away. And take heed to yourselves, lest at any time your hearts be overcharged with surfeiting, and drunkenness, and cares of this life, and so that day come upon you unawares. For as a snare shall it come on all them that dwell on the face of the whole earth. Watch ye therefore, and pray always, that ye may be accounted worthy to escape all these things that shall come to pass, and to stand before the Son of man. Luke 21:33-36 (KJV)

We will obtain what we pursue or what has us: is it God and the things of God, or does Satan have your heart with all the elements of death and hell.

The light of God's Word goes out of a complacent, wicked, and wayward heart because a person abandons truth and won't search it out.

And that which fell among thorns are they, which, when they have heard, go forth, and are choked with cares and riches and pleasures of this life, and bring no fruit to perfection. Luke 8:14 (KJV)

People look for things that they think will satisfy them; what a great thing to find satisfaction in God and live it. This is what the Word of God can give us.

MEN IN GENERAL LIVE OUT COMPLACENCY TOWARD GOD'S WORD; THEREFORE, THE LAMP GOES OUT BECAUSE OF COMPLACENCY, WICKEDNESS, AND THE WAYWARD HEART. WE MUST SEE WHEN AND WHERE THIS IS HAPPENING, SO WE CAN PREVENT COMPLACENCY'S CLOSURE OF ENTRY INTO GOD'S BLESSING AND WILL. WE MUST REVERSE IT BY FORCING OURSELVES TO GET BACK TO THE BIBLE. LET'S NOT HESITATE TO CALL ON GOD TO HELP US. WE MUST NOT BECOME A VICTIM OF FAILING TO ENTER INTO FELLOWSHIP WITH GOD BECAUSE WE WOULD NOT READ THE BIBLE.

With prayer and dialogue with God established through proper study, we can manage any being given over to the hindrances that cause us to fail to study, with God's help.

Blessed is the man that walketh not in the counsel of the ungodly, nor standeth in the way of sinners, nor sitteth in the seat of the scornful. But his delight is in the law of the LORD; and in his law doth he meditates day and night. And he shall be like a tree planted by the rivers of water, that bringeth forth his fruit in his season; his leaf also shall not wither; and whatsoever he doeth shall prosper. Psalm 1:1-3 (KJV)

The psalmist tells us if we will stand in God's counsel, we will meditate on God's Word. We cannot remove the Holy Spirit with his anointing from God's holy Word. It doesn't work. Both planting God's Word and our walk with God are necessary for optimal growth regularly. For our own value system, scripture is the authoritative rule. This is the pattern we follow, and use, to do God's Will, and bidding. Training in scripture is essential, we need to seek God for the blessing with it, and the opportunity to learn and apply it. Scripture is worth our most worthy zeal and cost to live it and know it; it points to Jesus. Through study, scripture becomes our leadership models, which we live out for our and others benefits. Any person who has started to study will quickly learn that God is more important than all other people or topics. We are given spiritual authority to help our own out of ruts.

We, as individuals, must study to know gospel truth, to drive truth through complacency to obtain freedom in Jesus Christ. As an individual, it's up to us (you and me) to dialogue within ourselves and speak truth as to view life correctly and have vision and purpose. Within human relationships, we have to stand for our faith: scripture helps us immensely here. We don't attack or violate others. God is not pleased if we contend to see how good we are, how better we are than someone else, or do damage to other people to get our way. That is nonsense in God's kingdom, for we are servant leaders; to be first, we must be last. Talk to God over your Christianity. Ask him for boldness, insight, and discernment as you read scripture; so, you can move in his guidance and convince others for Jesus.

The truth becomes especially important in times of crisis. We as individuals must recognize a satanic set-up when we see it. If we are not practicing the habit of studying scripture, then our thinking can become corrupted and our soil is spoiled, and our hearts will be led astray. The unhealthy reaction is to leave it that way: get alone and ask God to help you change what-ever it is. Identify what happened and the truth in it; declare that truth. Speak bible admonition to it.

The value of having study down and practicing it regularly is that you have a dialogue, new language going or building within: And the Holy Spirit will work within, utilizing that dialogue and language to speak through you in handling great problems of life. When a major problem arises, the Holy Spirit will announce it to your mind and tongue. You speak it to the problem, and God can work through the Word with his Holy Spirit anointing and that Word to the things that are going on.

WE SEE CERTAIN THINGS IN LUKE 6:45-46. INFLUENCE OF THE LIGHT OF GOD'S WORD GOES OUT. FIRST FROM WITHIN, FROM A COMPLACENCY AND WICKEDNESS OF A WAYWARD HEART.

People love sin, and choose darkness over light, and yield to the carnal nature; these people have abandoned God and his plan for them. Upon encountering the sins of the world, people feel they are entitled to that junk. Many people will make a total abandonment of truth within communities. Every level we find ourselves in, we find apostasy is marching on to total destruction. God's plan is allowed to be overridden by the world, but only because this is the end times scenario.

Society has been allowed to fester in sin, to throw out God, and the children are always the ones who suffer. By people putting God out of their lives, they invite apostasy, reprobation, and evil. People think they are free apart from God, but they are slaves to sin and death. People who give up God Will ultimately pay the eternal price because this is what they strive for, eternal death by being separated from God forever.

As individual's take initiative to hear, obey, and apply God's Word: we will be productive according to the Psalmist.

Blessed is the man that walketh not in the counsel of the ungodly, nor standeth in the way of sinners, nor sitteth in the seat of the scornful. But his delight is in the law of the LORD; and in his law doth he meditates day and night. And he shall be like a tree planted by the rivers of water, that bringeth forth his fruit in his season; his leaf also shall not wither; and whatsoever he doeth shall prosper. Psalm 1:1-3 (KJV)

We have also a surer word of prophecy; whereunto ye do well that ye take heed, as unto a light that shineth in a dark place, until the day dawn, and the day star arise in your hearts: 2 Peter 1:19 (KJV)

This verse tells us to take heed to the scripture teaching until the end, when light shines in our hearts again. As we look at scripture, it points to Jesus Christ. Our consciences bear witness with us as we direct it according to the Holy Word of God. Theology suggests we attentively study to gain precious insight for our lives and eternities perspective.

We, as individuals, must lay studying scripture to heart for our benefit. Praying over a prepared study is vital: for God alone can assure a worthy journey in life according to the Word. As we read, continually look for the application of scripture to yourself in life. We need God in seeking his way in life using scripture, prayer, and any other help. Pray that God will make a way for you.

IT IS CRITICAL WE REALIZE THAT OUT OF THE ABUNDANCE OF THE HEART COMES EITHER GOOD OR EVIL.

For a good tree bringeth not forth corrupt fruit; neither doth a corrupt tree brings forth good fruit. For every tree is known by his own fruit. For of thorns men do not gather figs, nor of a bramble bush gather they grapes. A good man out of the good treasure of his heart bringeth forth that which is good, and an evil man out of the evil treasure of his heart bringeth forth that which is evil: for of the abundance of the heart his mouth speaketh. And why call ye me, Lord, Lord, and do not the things which I say? Luke 6:43-46 (KJV)

The human heart produces either good or evil because if we have good things stored in our hearts, then we have good to share.

If we use scripture to edify ourselves and hide God's Word within; we store good in the heart and, thus, make it ready to serve God. The verse speaks of "A good man." He who is good. And it tells us, "Out of the good treasure." This comes from the person's reservoir of resources. He, "brings forth what is good." This is he who stores good in his heart by studying God's Holy Word. We have to give the Holy Spirit things to work with by putting it in our heart through study. God is the one who enables us to do his will.

We must spend time putting in our program of the diet of God's Word. As we study scripture, we have what we need. Then, as we go our way, the Holy Spirit can work through the small deposit we put in our heart.

The human heart produces either good or evil because if we have evil things stored in our hearts, then we will bring evil things forth.

If we are evil men who disregard God's Word, evil will manifest out of our hearts. The verse tells us, "An evil man," stores all manner of ungodliness (no God) in his heart and it manifests. The evil man, "bringeth forth that which is evil." What you put in your heart will come out.

If you're constantly putting evil in your heart; garbage in and garbage out; it will be what comes out of you which defiles you. What comes out shows what is within. If there is a young man cursing up a storm, it is because a spirit got in and is now manifesting.

Watch what goes in and what goes out. Either what we store in us can defile you or lead to service before God. Seek God over what goes in and out because God can save your tongue as well.

The human heart produces either good or evil because out of our obedience springs forth either good in us or the evil.

The treasure we set our heart on is that which possesses us, and it flows out of the mouth. The verse speaks of abundance. Which, in this particular context, means something other than God's Will is coming out of the heart. It means God is not the one we worship when out of our abundance evil comes forth as we have only deposited evil things within. How can an evil man say anything good? Unless there is a born-again experience, the Holy Spirit cannot work in one's heart yet and regenerate a person. Unless the person calls on Jesus to save them; they stay lost. Only as we look to Jesus can we be free; I truly believe the holy scripture points to Jesus in such a way.

Watch what comes in and goes out of your heart. Then you will have a say in your own wellbeing, as you trust God through Jesus. The prophet Daniel was so serious about what went into his heart, he caught the understanding that he should also be abstinent from unclean meat as well: he would not allow it to cause him to commit idolatry.

The human heart produces either good or evil because we cannot obey Jesus Christ according to his standard unless we are born again and enabled to through faith and obedience.

We cannot call Jesus Lord unless we become enlightened through a born again, regenerated life. Jesus asks us, "Why call me Lord?" Simply put, we do not belong to Jesus until we ask him to save us and commit our lives to his Lordship over us. He will enable us to obey him when we give him our life. If you never encountered Jesus, why call him Lord? Until Jesus changes you, you just pretend to follow him. For, "You do not do the things which I say." We cannot possibly do God's good will until the Holy Spirit lives within us through our born-again experience, where he puts God's good will and good ability in us.

Why pretend to be good without Jesus? Who will do God's will: is it the unbeliever, or the born-again man? It is he who gave himself over to Jesus and lets God work through himself.

Watch your heart because out of it comes the issues of life: and out of its abundance, the good or bad, proceed. Govern what goes into your heart and what goes out.

Chapter 2

The light of God's Word in other people

PEOPLE JUST DON'T CARE OR KNOW THE NEED TO APPLY SCRIPTURE TO WALK THEIR BEST WITH GOD.

People don't care to apply the Word of God to life because:

Many are searching for reality through experience instead of using scriptural truth for guidance. When one looks to experience, the assumption is that if I cannot see it, relate to it, and learn it in real life; they say it's phony. This experiential way of life has replaced scripture as one's guidance.

Many are searching for reality through experience through opinions as a viable level of truth, everyone's opinion being just as valid, and therefore why seek a biblical answer.

Many are searching for reality through experience and refuse to listen to avoid having God pushed on them. There are many who, for one reason or another, get all mad at the idea that "I have to follow and obey God?" To them, obeying and following God is about as criminally laden as any of the worst crimes.

Many are searching for reality through experience and don't accept a personal walk with God as possible, and therefore there is no need for scripture. For people who scorn, and don't believe there is no way to get the idea of personally knowing God, they simply won't try.

Many are searching for reality through experience and have no root in Jesus, thus, no perseverance, faith, experience or training in scripture. So, the bible is just a bizarre and complicated book which is unreachable for them. Many people shrink from bible study because there is no root in it for them.

<u>MOST PEOPLE, IN GENERAL, JUST DON'T CARE TO KNOW THE NEED TO APPLY SCRIPTURE TO WALK THEIR BEST WITH GOD. I HATE ASKING WHY THIS IS, BUT IT REVEALS ALL THE SATANIC ASSAULTS ON PEOPLE. WHY IS THIS HAPPENING? SATAN HAS PUT SUCH A BARRIER UP THAT PEOPLE WITHOUT GOD CANNOT GET THROUGH TO THE LIGHT AND GET THEIR VESSELS OILED UP FOR MEETING THE BRIDEGROOM IN THE RAPTURE. THE HELP THEY MUST ACQUIRE IS FOR A MENTOR TO TELL THEM, "SEEK GOD'S HELP FOR THE BREAK-THROUGH."</u>

You as a bible student and expert in study will have to lay groundwork to motivate and point out the possibilities of biblical freedom. Scripture can make us wise unto salvation. God's mysterious ways of working through his people play a critical or important role. As mentees become open and aware of scripture truth, they become free. This freedom must be exercised for their growth and responsibility before God. Any certain thing the person studies can be their next ability to move forward in their walk with God. It is this move of God, as we faithfully grow in study; where God changes things through experiences, and we are primed to grow. Most real spiritual authorities will advise these things.

The goal for the person is to acquire inner fellowship with God for the Lord to direct their heart.

Behold, the days come, saith the LORD, that I will make a new covenant with the house of Israel, and with the house of Judah: Not according to the covenant that I made with their fathers in the day that I took them by the hand to bring them out of the land of Egypt; which my covenant they brake, although I was an husband unto them, saith the LORD: But this shall be the covenant that I will make with the house of Israel; After those days, saith the LORD, I will put my law in their inward parts, and write it in their hearts; and will be their God, and they shall be my people. And they shall teach no more every man his neighbor, and every man his brother, saying, Know the LORD: for they shall all know me, from the least of them unto the greatest of them, saith the LORD: for I will forgive their iniquity, and I will remember their sin no more. Jeremiah 31:31–34 (KJV)

With this before us, we see God wants to take the wheel and direct all our lives. If we don't give sufficient time to him in prayer and study, then we give him nothing to work with in our lives. The Lord, now, will lead you to stand for truth. He will work his compassion in you for others. Talk to God and seek his direction for intuition: ask God, "Please

Lord, help me know what to do and do it." If anyone asks, "give me a way."

But sanctify the Lord God in your hearts: and be ready always to give an answer to every man that asketh you a reason of the hope that is in you with meekness and fear: 1 Peter 3:15 (KJV)

This verse tells people the hope with in us. Why we serve God within the situation (God's making process) or despite the situation (He who endures to the end will be saved). Each community we are a part of has an atmosphere. Remember: use principles for community and proclamation over the atmosphere: you take personal responsibility over both to steward them godly. Use your Mission, Vision, and Values in the community: and the Word of God spoken in the atmosphere. Give godly hospitality and leadership to the people. Administer justly and don't demeanor your enemy. Leave judgment to God. Pass your test, both outer and inner ones. Seek God to do it. Talk to God and explain your actions, expecting God's help with interaction and interposing. Give place for his intervention.

Freedom is hard won. Once earned, keep the trust, or you'll lose it. You be responsible with your freedom to do all in your power to be responsible and godly, then thank God.

OTHER PEOPLE WHO WON'T READ OR USE SCRIPTURE; PROBABLY BECAUSE THEY ARE UNBELIEVERS OR A BELIEVER IN NAME ONLY; THESE TYPES OF PEOPLE HAVE NO CLUE OF SCRIPTURE'S POWER TO HELP AND MAKE A PERSON WISE UNTO SALVATION.

Some people are content to live life without using the bible and are happy to find human solutions to life. Naturalists who deal with life without God are these types. God allows things to happen to draw us into a real and deeper walk with him. Without scripture such a walk is harder learned, toils get hard. This hits home with us, but without the Word of God, life's tests have less meaning, and we are left wondering what God's will is.

Why does it take so long to pick up our bible and learn to trust God? People would rather trust Satan and assume he gave them the presents that came from God. It's bad enough to learn through hardships, but to go through them and attribute your victory to Satan is to live a lie and total defeat.

You shall find God when you search for him with all your heart. Searching God out is our privilege and joy in life-do it. Probably we realize, "There is a God." But what does he have to do with me? This is what scripture teaches us. God will communicate if we give him something to work with.

Seek, ask, and knock for Jesus and God will give him to you. Why not ask God yourself for His life through Jesus and the knowledge of his Word. These people can read scripture and without the Holy Spirit in their hearts, no revelation will come forth. So, get into a position God can give you knowledge in scripture.

WE CAN SERVE JESUS ACCEPTABLY BEFORE GOD THROUGH THE APPLICATION OF SCRIPTURE.

But if thy brother be grieved with thy meat, now walkest thou not charitably. Destroy not him with thy meat, for whom Christ died. Let not then your good be evil spoken of: For the kingdom of God is not meat and drink, but righteousness, and peace, and joy in the Holy Ghost. For he that in these things serveth Christ is acceptable to God, and approved of men. Let us therefore follow after the things which make for peace, and things wherewith one may edify another. Romans 14:15–19 (KJV)

Scripture teaches us how to avoid hurting others. Just as other people who are indifferent to us, in our beliefs towards our neighbors; we tend to mis-the-mark with uncharitableness. It is God's Word which teaches us to love each other. "If thy brother be grieved," says the scriptures. We cannot let our liberties ruin other people's faith. Our passage shows us scripture expresses that we build up God's family. We have had persons in our life which we cared about and loved; we are to do this with all. Develop loving and godly relationships. Ask God to establish his Word as the pattern of charity within you. We must learn to serve Jesus acceptable using scripture.

Scripture guides us to guard our walk in the Spirit. We must prioritize God first in our life. Make staying in step with the Holy Spirit our goal for four reasons: 1. To make sure good is not evil spoken of, 2. God's Kingdom is not meat and drink, 3. The Kingdom of God is righteousness, peace, and joy, and 4. All in the Holy Spirit.

The verse tells us to let not our good be evil spoken of. We must stand for that Word obeyed before God. Also, "The Kingdom is not meat and drink." God's kingdom is so much greater than earthly created pleasures and necessities. Furthermore, as we abide with the Holy Spirit, we will find that in him, we are in Jesus and in the Kingdom of God.

It is our privilege to be in Christ, walk with God, love him, and obey. We are to guard the good deposit of Christ in us! The scriptures applied help us follow God the Spirit and not contradict him.

There is a thing to be guarded: 1. Our walk in the Spirit of God, 2. Viewing and pursuing God's Kingdom rightly, 3. Standing for godliness. Also, we must protect biblical character. This is how we serve God acceptably using scripture.

Scripture helps us serve Jesus acceptably in divine approval. As people of freedom, we can take God's Word and learn to live with God's approval. "In these things," means to avoid hurting others and walking in the Spirit and be accepted by God. The verse says that we serve Christ. Without God's Word, we simply don't know these things. Anyone in validity and truth; by God through the Word can serve God and others. When we begin and learn to serve God: we will find God's Word becomes the ultimate dimension with which to draw motivation.

We each can be motivated to do God's Will and bidding. It's a choice, and we can choose to use scripture to guide us in it. By serving God using scripture and God's Word, we can impact for God.

Scripture shows us the way of peace and edification. We are to attempt to stay and be at peace with our follow man. The verse tells us to follow those things that make for peace utilizing scripture. Scripture will show us this. If we are led by God and the Holy Scripture, then we have ways to edify and establish peace and build others up.

If you are not driven by scripture to edify and make peace, then pick up the bible. Using scripture makes all the difference. Scripture will show you the way of planting for peace.

Chapter 3

The light of God's Word in families

FAMILIES HAVE BEEN DEVASTATED BY SATAN WITH A COMPLETE REMOVAL OF THE LIGHT OF GOD'S WORD; MAKING MOST FAMILIES NONFUNCTIONAL AND BROKEN.

Those families who have abandoned seeking God are usually void of doing bible study together. When there is no Word studied and applied in our hearts to keep us in any of our ways, anything goes. When anything goes, God's ways go, and so does our ability to stay together.

Those families who have abandoned seeking God together using scripture don't have the value of spiritual disciplines established within them, so they become prey to all sorts of invading belief systems. Without a base laid of godly instruction, we become penetrated by every wind of doctrine and make ourselves subject to such foul thinking.

Those families who have abandoned seeking God together using scripture seek raising children devoid of any biblical mentorship and its godly influence in their lives. These people set themselves and their families up for failure, "and everyone did what was right in his own eyes."

Those families who have abandoned seeking God together using scripture find as storms of life blow on their families that their lives constantly fall apart. When this happens, usually the family doesn't stand together anymore.

Satan has devastated families with a complete removal of the light of God's Word. This has made most families nonfunctional and broken. We know a family is in trouble when it has totally abandoned seeking God through his Word. It is critical, if you will save your family, to plead with God to set your house in order and establish godly habits.

Parents have to put life in focus and set habits aright. Sacrifice is in order: what do we bring to God in which he can use to make a difference? We see the Holy Spirit gifting a young boy with a lunch, which he gave to Jesus, that Jesus may take it and feed thousands of people. Our goal in sacrifice is long-term change in our family. A lifeline of preparing ourselves through godliness training by God's Word and offering ourselves to God, giving him tangible habits, he can and will bless which we align with his will through prayer. Parents must lead the modeling of such steps to progress and teach their children and to live that way. This pattern will teach the children the character and enablement to make godly things happen. Parents are the authority which empowers their children to trust God for great things. God will be the one who performs the miracles.

Here is the formula: 1. God has primacy over the family (all in the family commits to it). 2. Long-term sacrifice accepted. 3. The gamble equals the potential for all.

Have the family commit to God. Put out any enemy's thought of deterrence. Stand for God's place in our family. Be nice and don't violate one another, praying to God on behalf of one another. So, we accept that God is over our family, and we commit to it. Satan will strike at this by the gates of hell. Satan will attempt to get you or someone else to break the commitment through getting mad, capitulating, or some other thing. It's time to go back to the beginning and remember that a vow was made to our God. Return to God.

Realize that the gates of hell move to take such a commitment from God. Recommit to God's sovereignty and his purpose for the family. Speak God's Lordship and oversight in the family atmosphere, and have each assemble and pray over each person and God's Word in the atmosphere. They will become leaders. Let the parents encourage the children and declare war on Satan. Renew and speak blessing into each one's commitment to God. Thank God and declare his love, will, and ways over the family. Let each member learn to take charge in facilitating prayer and God's will.

Our families live as if there were no God. The bible is just a good book. No-one left a mark or example for people to follow by reading the book. The bible, now out of the public domain, and out of schools-no one teaches the people to read it: so, they stay free thinkers, and never hope in God. All this is happening in America with rapid growth in crime, pregnancies in school, guns and violence as part of the scene. Had the children had parents who read scripture, this would probably be dealt with. But no time with kids means we refuse to love them. Yes, we provide, but is that all love is?

This isn't just a societal problem, but individuals refuse to get this right and support their families by the Word and prayer. Without a mentor, we won't see people read the bible and how faith is lived out. Instead, the hope is lost and so is biblical love for others. Because of the hopelessness our children have, we are obligated to share the Word with them, so they can acquire Jesus and God's Word for themselves.

Teach your children because it is our job and not the public schools. Study to show thyself approved. Exhort one another as you see the day approaching. Without the reading of scripture, our consciences will condemn us for not seeking God regularly. If we don't read, we lose our vision: he who has more will be given; to him who does not have, even what he has will be taken away from him. Mk 4:25. My suggestion is that we read and study. Start your study asking God to bless you.

<u>It is critical we use scripture to govern our homes.</u>

One that ruleth well his own house, having his children in subjection with all gravity;

(For if a man knows not how to rule his own house, how shall he take care of the church of God?)

Not a novice, lest being lifted up with pride he falls into the condemnation of the devil.

Moreover, he must have a good report of them which are without; lest he fall into reproach and the snare of the devil. **1 Timothy 3:4-7 (KJV)**

We must use scripture to govern our homes because God uses our training in his Word to help the children to be in subject to authority in all godliness.

Our families are precious to God and the future state of the nation. As we rule our houses, we teach our children how to model godliness, leadership, family devotions, love, scripture training, etc. Ours is a job to show a Christlike life before our children. We are commanded to be those who ruleth well our houses. We must model Christian leadership before our family. We are to do this with gravity (serious or dignified behavior; by Random House Webster's Unabridged Dictionary). Ruling without corruption. To rule God's house, then we must first rule our house well. The way we model Jesus Christ is the way we train our children to follow and obey authority and live godly lives. What we are after is to train up our children to imitate Jesus in any community they find themselves in. Let's give scripture a place in our lives as families again in devotional time together. This will bless our family with fresh and new hope. We set precedents in our families to edify, build up and establish godly order.

We must use scripture to govern our homes because through proper training God teaches the spiritual leader to avoid pride.

We have to get to a place before God when pride does not drive us anymore. If it's all about us, it's a pride issue. Seek God until it is gone. We are commanded not to be a novice. We must not let our guard down. Verse 6 tells us being lifted one might fall into condemnation of the devil. Any preacher can get proud if he hasn't prayed through. The preacher can think he or she is the reason everything is working; they really need God. This situation with pride is the same with parents; they must seek God to shoot their arrows and hit the mark. Dads can look at the children's good side and say, "Cut off the same block," but God alone is the reason the child is seeking God. Let's avoid pride by using scripture to acquire God's favor in his presence. That's what spiritual disciplines are for; coming before God, through a spiritual discipline, to obtain unmerited favor.

We must use scripture to govern our homes because God can teach the spiritual leader of the house to keep a good report, to avoid reproach, and avoid the snare of the devil.

A father must be known as a leader and have a reputation as a good father figure and head of his house. God through his Word can make that happen through the father as he yields himself to God. So, we got to have a good report. The Father should be like a bishop, having a good report of his modeling in his family's house. We are also told to avoid the snare of the devil. Without a good report, evil can overwhelm the father. By daily using scripture to seek God and his will, God will teach his plans to him. Scripture fully equips us for why God calls a family. The father can clean what is needed by preparing himself.

Chapter 4

The light of God's Word in the Church

WITHIN THE CHURCH, THERE IS GREAT DISSENTION OVER GOD'S WORD: WHERE WE CAME FROM IN TRUTH AND WHERE WE ARE GOING.

The Church without bible origins, Church history, Western history, knowledge of death, judgment, heaven and hell leaves its citizens out there.

A Church without bible origins causes us to have little diligence for study. Only a few elitists have it. We need a whole education again and the vision and purpose for which we derive our desire to excel for God.

A Church without bible origins causes us to except haphazard study. An approach without discipline in study and without anyone to teach us. We will, at best, only be mediocre! We have not accepted, "The best education we can get."

A Church without bible origins leaves us unable to relate to the times of the day we live in. The people of the congregation don't have enough of the Word to discern what's going on in our day. They don't know their baton is being passed to someone else. This kind of congregation has become a Sunday social club and their purpose for being will be removed.

A Church without bible origins leaves the members thinking it's all about them and what they want. They get so busy doing their own will that God's will and purpose fall to the ground. These people have a drive and drive themselves right out of God's will. Eventually, they crash in useless agenda.

THE CHURCH RESIDES IN A PLATEAU WHERE THERE IS GREAT DISSENTION OVER GOD'S WORD, AND WHERE WE CAME FROM IN TRUTH, WHERE WE ARE GOING, AND WHO IS THE TRUE CHURCH. CONFUSION, CHAOS, AND LACK OF EDIFICATION IN CONFESSION IS SATAN'S ATTEMPT TO QUENCH GOD'S FLAME. THIS IS A CONCERN FOR ALL. WHEN THE CHURCH DIVIDES INSTEAD OF UNITES US IN JESUS; OVERHAUL IS NEEDED AND QUICK, SOMETHING MUST BE DONE.

The Church sets the standard for the bibles place in people's lives. If the bible is removed, so is the setting from which the Holy Spirit resides. This is important for us to retain God's move in our lives.

Thou therefore, my son, be strong in the grace that is in Christ Jesus.

And the things that thou hast heard of me among many witnesses, the same commit thou to faithful men, who shall be able to teach others also. **2 Timothy 2:1-2 (KJV)**

The Holy Spirit is the one who takes scripture and causes anointed movement and godly manifestation with our hearts, lives, and within the community we are a part of. The Church is the gauge and monitoring tool for God's Word within society: if God's light goes out with her, society suffers. The Church trains her people to know how to read and study, and practice good habits. The leaders are seers appointed to guide the Church community to forward progress through biblical means. The greatest experience the Church could hope God would give her is the members excelling in their intimate walk with God. Overseers model the way, so the members can follow behind.

To the Church community: If we will get to our destination, we must fuel up daily with God's Word; God won't use an empty vessel. We must be able to dialogue as a community honestly about when and how we stand on God's precepts and Word. The goal is to break through our indifference to high motivation in God's Word, the Kingdom, in community, and as all these things apply to our lives. Will we cordially work through the complacency without tearing each other apart? The Lord helps us make progress on the path lighted by the fire of his Word: this needs to be whispered in the prayer meetings of our congregations.

We need to declare the biblical truth because God cares and loves us and will guide us to the promised pasture where he can minister his presence to us. Don't allow the temporary situation to guide you! You direct the atmosphere by speaking the Word of God to it. God's hand is in the whole thing. Try, to exercise faith, obey God and the Word which will do miracles in you. May God deal with the ones who try to remove

God from you. Stay the course. God guide us, help us and restore us. Help us know what to do and to do it. May we collaborate for the community to be faithful reading, studying, loving God, and cherishing his Word.

WHAT IS GOING ON IN THE CHURCH? THIS IS WHERE THE WORD OF GOD SHOULD THRIVE, BUT, UNFORTUNATELY, COMPLACENCY IS SETTING IN ON HER DESIRE TO READ, LEARN, KNOW, AND UTILIZE SCRIPTURE FOR HER STRUGGLES.

The Church has taken a position of attempting to minister to God and others without being saturated in scripture. Instead, she has removed scripture from God's Holy presence within her meetings. Afraid scripture will scare away the people: this attitude removes the Holy Spirit from his setting in scripture. This forces God away from such Churches. People come to receive. If we don't share the Word, they don't get anything at all: far worse to come and leave empty. When individuals should share Christ's victory and encourage one another; now they soothe each other's wounds of defeat (because they attempt to live and do life without God's instructions).

Not everyone that saith unto me, Lord, Lord, shall enter into the kingdom of heaven; but he that doeth the will of my Father which is in heaven. Many will say to me in that day, Lord, Lord, have we not prophesied in thy name? and in thy name have cast out devils? and in thy name done many wonderful works? And then will I profess unto them, I never knew you: depart from me, ye that work iniquity. Therefore, whosoever heareth these sayings of mine, and doeth them, I will liken him unto a wise man, which built his house upon a rock: And the rain descended, and the floods came, and the winds blew, and beat upon that house;

and it fell not: for it was founded upon a rock. And every one that heareth these sayings of mine, and doeth them not, shall be likened unto a foolish man, which built his house upon the sand: And the rain descended, and the floods came, and the winds blew, and beat upon that house; and it fell: and great was the fall of it. Matthew 7:21-27 (KJV)

This passage gives clear admonition to hear and build on Jesus. If we don't, then destruction happens. People attempt to build their houses without God's Word, and it leaves their efforts devastated. What is left when it's all done: divorce, broken lives, broken spirits, etc. We want to get to the heart of the issue: people are living without the bible (basic instructions before leaving earth). Without the bible, it won't work.

Those who will be great in God's domain live and teach God's commands.

The bible is a leadership manual on how to hear, obey, and follow through on God's Will and commands. Our personal righteousness is measured by how we read, learn, and apply the Word of God. Yes, we need Jesus Christ's righteousness, but reading scripture gives us time before God when he can work through, using our devotion for that day. He works through our effort with his abilities; this is a big difference.

Seek God's will to obey daily. What are you wanting of me today, Oh Lord? Let's ask this in our preparations. Let's align ourselves with policies encouraging scripture reading within the Church. Why don't you start a bible study group?

<u>OUR COMMITMENT IS ESSENTIAL TO OUR ZEALOUS FERVENCY.</u>

And unto the angel of the church of the Laodiceans write; These things saith the

Amen, the faithful and true witness, the beginning of the creation of God; I know thy works, that thou art neither cold nor hot: I would thou wert cold or hot. So then because thou art lukewarm, and neither cold nor hot, I will spue thee out of my mouth. Because thou sayest, I am rich, and increased with goods, and have need of nothing; and knowest not that thou art wretched, and miserable, and poor, and blind, and naked: I counsel thee to buy of me gold tried in the fire, that thou mayest be rich; and white raiment, that thou mayest be clothed, and that the shame of thy nakedness does not appear; and anoint thine eyes with eye salve, that thou mayest see. As many as I love, I rebuke and chasten: be zealous therefore, and repent. Behold, I stand at the door, and knock: if any man hears my voice, and open the door, I will come in to him, and will sup with him, and he with me. To him that overcometh will I grant to sit with me in my throne, even as I also overcame, and am set down with my father in his throne. He that hath an ear, let him hear what the Spirit saith unto the churches. Revelation 3:14-22 (KJV)

Our commitment is essential to our zealous fervency because Jesus Christ is the one, we either please or turn off.

God addresses all Churches as its head. He knows us and our works, and if we are truly his or just going through the motions. We must stay betrothed and in love with Jesus. The initial stirring of the Spirit in us at salvation is ok, but we have to commit and stir our own love up for Jesus. The verses stress, "because you are lukewarm…," Someone is neither hot nor cold. The verse goes on to say, "I will spew thee out!" That kind of dedication is repugnant, and God will eject you. This is a laze-fair attitude and half-hazard dedication. God's looking for men and women fully given to his will and love. Continue to turn back to God's Word. Let's give God ourselves while we have time.

Our commitment is essential to our zealous fervency because our fervent love toward Jesus Christ determines our riches and true spiritual health.

This Laodicean Church thought that they were rich, but were poor in God's eyes. Their riches were more important than pursuing God. "Because thou sayest, I am rich and immersed with goods." This Laodicean Church thought more of her riches and goods than the condition of her heart. Jesus said also, "I counsel thee." Jesus set out to change her outcome, but she would not love Jesus' gift of life, but her goods. This is typical of end time Churches today because when they hit it big, they take success over relationship with Jesus. It all comes down to choosing: what will you do with Jesus Christ? Each of us is deciding.

How does our Church and each of us do? Is the Church choosing life through Jesus or all the goods flowing from him? Is our Church about gain, or knowing Jesus? If that is the case, let's turn to scripture and find out how Calvary's love defeated such a material spirit!

Our commitment is essential to our zealous fervency because Jesus Christ knocks and corrects us so that we would walk with him and stay in his fellowship.

Jesus corrects us because he loves us, and therefore we repent and stay in fellowship with God. Jesus is at our door, pleading that we open to him and have fellowship. Jesus said, "As many as I love, I rebuke." God will straighten out his people. Jesus tells us, "I stand at the door." Jesus begs for us to open our heart's door. Let us receive God's Word, which points to Jesus. This points to how we view and trust God's sword (the Word), which is how we trust and treat God.

We are to accept testimony of scripture of Jesus Christ and let him be our God in fellowship. Give our self to God. Let that fellowship guide our way of life.

Our commitment is essential to our zealous fervency because faith in Jesus Christ and motivation to overcome are both given as we hear the Spirit speak and lead us.

The Spirit testifies of Jesus Christ and we with him. If we overcome, we will be rulers with Jesus in his Kingdom. This all occurs as we continue in faith, led by God's Spirit. The scripture describes the one who overcomes as receiving a challenge: Let Jesus govern us, listen to the Spirit, and be on fire for God. We can only do this if the Spirit brings scripture to the altar of our hearts where it burns in our heart and strengthening love in us for God. Regenerating and sanctifying us in Jesus. We are to, "Let him hear what the Spirit saith unto the Church." Our job is to listen to the Spirit and obey him.

Open up to God and the power of God as noted in scripture. Let God have his way. God will take you to the next level of faith, fellowship, obedience, and our purpose in life.

Chapter 5
The light of God's Word in learning societies

IRONICALLY, BIBLICAL TRUTH IS FROWNED UPON OR REMOVED IN MOST LEARNING CENTERS, AND THEY HAVE BECOME BATTLEGROUNDS TO DESTROY BELIEVERS AND THEIR FAITH.

When a higher learning center puts bible truth out, then the people in those societies are under managed agenda. They feel it's their job to de-indoctrinate believers and reform their beliefs by educated agendas.

It is my opinion that in most higher learning centers, there is hate for God, the believers, faith, and other things. As soon as a person of faith enters, the target is placed on them and the painful changing process is underway.

When a higher learning center puts bible truth out, it is because there is a great fight against traditional faith. These centers hate what traditional Christians stand for. The progressive move is to remove God and anything about him.

As higher learning centers put bible truth out, propaganda and indoctrination go on to blind people of belief. The horrendous campaign of these centers works to blind and incorporate the innocent into an army of secular humanist.

When higher learning centers put bible truth out, such things as Naturalism, Gnosticism, Evolutionism, and Atheism are taught. This is the only rational idea of the origins of mankind-existence of life without God: absurd completely.

When higher learning centers put bible truth out, it becomes enlightenment and rationalistic driven. No longer is the bible the dominant influence; instead, they teach the godhood of man and humanistic reasoning as the highest level of intelligence.

As higher learning centers move forward with their agenda's occultic like enemies emerge to fight all believers. You wouldn't believe the diversity of people they will choose who step up and fight with hate, all who represent Jesus Christ. They are a unity-through-diversity of God haters.

WITHIN HIGHER LEARNING CENTERS, TRUTH IS REMOVED, AND THEY HAVE BECOME BATTLEGROUNDS TO DESTROY BELIEVERS AND THEIR FAITH.

Enter any community college, and immediately you will since a wall of evil against believers. It will in time manifest in a battle or war against us. Do not be a hell-raiser because it will grow worse. Instead, lay it out before God. Trust and listen to God and obey his solution.

The individual's attending at these higher learning centers, which battle for the place of occupancy within the souls of the students, can endure it if they stay kinetically committed to God's call on their life. Meeting in groups develops networks and support. They can then give and receive edification and support in their walk with God. The Holy Spirit's leading is paramount for success. He has to be invited in and attended to. Bible groups can achieve that. The spirit dominating the pathway is greed and material centered. Gnosticism, Atheism, Secular Humanism, Naturalism, and others are all part of the spirits wandering the halls in these education centers. Let Calgary penetrate the malevolent spirits. These and other tactical and strategic spirits and their beliefs are diabolic, demonic, and heretical. Learn to identify and ward off that kind of thinking. Calvary's love is the only way to safely resist the enemy. Vigilance is so important to make it through the long haul, but so is continuance and diligence. Experience tells us this, that tomorrow will bring our next battle, but God will be faithful. Let's remember God's sovereignty over us, and thus, submit to him.

When you're in, learning societies, keep your inner dialogue under control, so you keep peace in your outer dialogue. You will have to declare your position before people. That is your place of declaring Jesus Christ as your Lord and Savior. Work in good faith with a pleasant attitude. Don't start battles against people if necessary. Express to God the help you need. Say to God, your servant is among hungry lions.

In order for a Christian to speak any truth, they may have to go before a firing squad, so-to-speak. The Christian may have to do that today, speaking for Christ is that urgent. Someone is going to start something with a Christian, and we are not to back down. Backing down and assuming to accept being a victim as acceptable will only bring you to a victim status. Getting an attitude never helps with dealing with persecution. Figure out what truth must be spoken and speak it. Don't be afraid.

IRONICALLY, BIBLE TRUTH IS REMOVED IN MOST LEARNING SOCIETIES, AND THEY HAVE BECOME BATTLEGROUNDS TO DESTROY BELIEVERS AND THEIR FAITH.

Once you are known as a Christian, a hidden target is placed on you. The hidden enemy summons his agents and they start shooting at any belief or faith you may have. The goal is to make Christians look like idiots as they share their belief. They are continuously set up to fail so that they dump their religious belief in Jesus Christ. You might find yourself in a university or a Community College with teachers with doctorates fully indoctrinated in evolution and secular humanism. If you're lucky, you'll find yourself in a college that may have religious courses, if not, you may have to kiss your beliefs goodbye.

People don't want to serve God anymore, they say, "No God." If people question you, it's not because they want to learn that they may change. Rather, those who question do so that they may know how to drive your belief out. Their problem in fault-finding tactics is to avoid being condemned, so they don't have to conform to Jesus; whom they don't want to serve that they may stay in sin.

Scripture tells us scoffers will come in the last days, telling us, "What happened to the promise of his coming?" This is a rejection of bible truth and readiness. They have forgotten all of this world is reserved for the judgment of fire, swiftly approaching. Let's continue in faith, though all others walk away; surely this is where the true battle is. Persevere in God's grace because he who endures to the end shall be saved.

Hold fast your crown until the end. Daily, pray through your struggles and contentions. Seek what the bible says about your situation. If you lack certain reference resources, then now is the time to obtain them.

<u>IT IS CRITICAL, WE ARE RESPONSIBLE FOR THE COMING MALEVOLENT VILIFICATION OF CHRISTIANS WITHIN OUR SOCIETIES.</u>

Again the word of the LORD came unto me, saying, Son of man, speak to the children of thy people, and say unto them, When I bring the sword upon a land, if the people of the land take a man of their coasts, and set him for their watchman: If when he seeth the sword come upon the land, he blow the trumpet, and warn the people; Then whosoever heareth the sound of the trumpet, and taketh not warning; if the sword come, and take him away, his blood shall be upon his own head. He heard the sound of the trumpet, and took not warning; his blood shall be upon him. But he that taketh warning shall deliver his soul. But if the watchman sees the sword come, and blow not the trumpet, and the people be not warned; if the sword come, and take any person from among them, he is taken away in his iniquity; but his blood will I require at the watchman's hand. So, thou, O son of man, I have set thee a watchman unto the house of Israel; therefore, thou shalt hear the word at my mouth, and warn them from me. When I say unto the wicked, O wicked man, thou shalt surely die; if thou dost not speak to warn the wicked from his way, that wicked man shall die in his iniquity; but his blood will I require at thine hand. Nevertheless, if thou warn the wicked of his way to turn from it; if he does not turn from his way, he shall die in his iniquity; but thou hast delivered thy soul. Ezekiel 33:1-9 (KJV)

An assembly is responsible for its own watchmen to protect its community (verse 1-2).

God warns each community of people to set guard for the protection of their communities and people. God tells the people, "When I bring a sword." God will test each community. When the verse tells us that when the community takes a man for a watchman, it means it is the community's responsibility to watch. So, the watcher blows the trumpet if danger comes: the task being to warn of what's coming.

It is a very high responsibility which the individual must have God's help to warn the people. A guard in the military serves such a purpose. Watch and warn; know our God and do as he say. We must constantly be in communication with God. The correct person can halt judgment, while the wrong person will hasten it.

A community of individuals are responsible for their own life when the alarm of danger is sounded (verses 3-5).

As an appointed watcher warns: each person is responsible for knowing what to do, doing it, and calling on God. The verse points out, "Whosoever heareth the sound." We must listen and respond. This makes each of us responsible for obeying. If you came across danger, you must handle it godly and responsibly.

You are to respond in the directed way. If you don't know the right way to handle it, then you must find out. If you will live, you must respond accordingly.

A community must hold its watchmen accountable for the welfare of its people (verse 6).

Here is the dilemma of the watchers; they must sound the alarm, or the blood of the people will be on their hands. This is why watchers cannot be shady people. If they do the bidding in their own interests and do not care who dies or the cost to them, then people will die.

The community must hold the watcher in either contempt toward the people, or in obedience to the people's wellbeing based on their action. For the community is putting everything on the line with these watchers. The watcher is also or must be responsible to God. For God will be the Judge.

Two-way responsibility is needed here: The people of the community must pick and keep credible men. Also, the individuals must be responsible and credible. All are observed and will come under God's Judgment.

God calls his followers to be watchmen over their communities to warn them (verse 7).

As a person answering God's call, we are responsible for hearing God's Word and giving warning to the people. The verse tells us, "I have set thee a watchman." God calls all his Harold's to obey in this way.

It's when God gives his Word, the word must be proclaimed. Some preachers think, "I hold it until I profit from it." That's not God's way. We don't share God's Word for profit.

We must share God's Word with people who need repentance; these are the ones God wants to save and incorporate in his work.

Just as the watcher give warning to the people to repent of their ways; they must choose to obey God's command (verses 8-9).

There is a dual responsibility here. Those giving the alarm must be equally responsible as those who receive the message. They each must do their part. The verse says, "when I say unto the wicked… and thou dost not speak to warn him." Our job is to hear God's Word and lay it out to the sinner. "If thou warn the wicked…if he does not turn from his way." You save yourself if you warn and the wicked does not turn.

This is the plight people choose. They can either obey God, or shut the door in his face. This is what's going on today. People here the warning and shut the door in God's face.

Warn and obey, or hear and obey, is God's demand from his call. Thus, it's necessary for the watchers to hear from God's Word and put it out to the people. Then we must abide by it.

Chapter 6

The light of God's Word in the believer

The believer has to be cautious and forthright in making sure that the light of God's Word continues to burn in his or her heart, life, program, growth, and testimony.

Caution is a must for believers to keep growing in God's Word because our enemies work to de-abilify us. De-abilify works to systematically break you down as soon as works of the faith life are perceived. As you work on it, enemies work to remove it.

Caution also is a must for believers to keep growing in God's Word because obstacles will cause us to be sidelined. Life comes through tests, obstacles, pressures, crisis's, trials, persecutions, etc. We have to seek God from their inception to their demise.

Caution is a must for believers to keep growing in God's Word because it's up to us to stir on our flame to study for growth. We can maintain against certain things, or see our testimony fall to the ground. We must add the ability to maintain. Growth, vision, direction, all come through seeking God in spiritual direction.

Caution is a must for believers to keep growing in God's Word because we need to recall the fervency of all mentors who helped us convert and grow in Jesus. To stay on the path. Our talents and desire must be fired up for service.

Caution is a must for believers to keep growing in God's Word because we must guard scripture anointing before it is systematically removed to stop influencing other people. If we stay in scripture study, God will supply all you're anointing.

Caution is a must for believers to keep growing in God's Word because we must avoid being complacency-driven. If we are satisfied (with the Christian life and setting) we won't do a thing. Our goal as a leader is to change the status quo.

<u>THE TRUE SITUATION IN THE BELIEVER.</u>

It is up to the believer to be cautious and forthright in making sure that the light of God's Word continues to burn in his or her heart, life, purpose, growth, and testimony.

If we are not studying the bible, it's time to put ourselves in motion. We must stay with it as we read until the scriptures come alive. We are going to have to deal with this. It's up to us to fan into flame our hunger for God and his Word.

Thy Word have I hid in my heart, that I might not sin against the Lord. We put

God's Word in us, so the Holy Spirit can pull it out through-out the day as a defense against the attacks waged against us. Without establishing verses, we can draw from; the enemy has an advantage. Meditate on small portions of scripture in the morning. Also, add to that regular bible reading: a schedule to read the bible within the year. Some years you accomplish this, and some years you only get a partial portion read. Do it anyway. Let scripture be your authoritative rule for life by the Holy Spirit's leading.

To protect our salvation: scripture should support our walk with God. Do not put your salvation on the line when a contender argues with you. Hide it in your heart. Stand by quoting verses and that's how you contend. Be nice and forthrightly declare your faith through verses as they apply. Talk to God and ask Him to give you the scripture verses.

Speak scripture in truth and in love, addressing the contender and the need in the situation, or anything anyone may need. Thank God through it all. Be an adult in how you approach contention.

WE-THE BELIEVERS: WE AS BELIEVERS HAVE TO LET GOD'S WORD PERMEATE EVERY AREA OF OUR LIFE.

We have to become mature in scripture to train other new believers while taking care of ourselves.

A lot rests on the individual Christian: spiritual warfare, obstacles, preparations, study, fervency, being alert against deceivers, etc. Studying and practicing godliness have to be at the forefront of all one does as a Christian, to walk in truth with God and model the Christian life for the new believer. When the challenges within the Christian community begin to take over one's ability to perform his purpose;

immediately, study has to be the result. We have to have our priorities and ministry in the forefront and biblically based, so we can exercise our trade within any community we find ourselves.

The nature of our world demands we be responsible individuals, so we have to work out our individual vision and purpose. Because scripture teaches Satan and the gates of hell where the Satanic world operates, we must learn to be vigilant and remain all God calls us to be. We are called peculiar because we are faithful to the unseen God. Everything about Him is our purpose in life.

We are to let our life conversation honor God, even before the people who hate us. Overcome evil with good and bear a cross even when it is arduous and hard. We must live our lives in a way our testimony is not nullified. Theology helps us address issues we might have no ability to handle. Study and pray. We must pray. We must pray when we are leading people, and God will help us. We have to get to a place we can live bearing our testimony among opposition.

<u>IT IS NECESSARY THAT MATURE BELIEVERS OF SCRIPTURE CHANGE THEIR WAYS.</u>

And the word of the LORD came unto me, saying, Son of man, prophesy against the shepherds of Israel, prophesy, and say unto them, thus saith the Lord GOD unto the shepherds; Woe *be* to the shepherds of Israel that do feed themselves! should not the shepherds feed the flocks? Ye eat the fat, and ye clothe you with the wool, ye kill them that are fed: *but* ye feed not the flock. The diseased have ye not strengthened, neither have ye healed that which was sick, neither have ye bound up *that which was* broken, neither have ye brought again that which was driven away, neither have ye sought that which was lost; but with force and with cruelty have ye ruled them. And they were scattered, because *there is* no shepherd: and they became meat to all the beasts of the field, when they were scattered. My sheep wandered through all the mountains, and upon every high hill: yea, my flock was scattered upon all the face of the earth, and none did search or seek *after them*. **Ezekiel 34:1-6 (KJV)**

Mature believers of scripture can change their ways by learning to give a word to help others instead of just pleasing themselves (verses 1-2).

God is concerned that believers can help others: if they can feed themselves, then they can encourage others with a word from God. The verse says that the Word of the Lord came unto Ezekiel.

We must receive God's Word as it comes to us. The word that came was woe to the shepherds that feed themselves. Here God tells us to give as we have received. This is for all believers, but especially under shepherds.

God is willing to use you to help other people. Share the Word, as you have received it, with other people. Give to others the gift of life-the gospel of Jesus Christ.

Mature believers of scripture can change their ways by feeding the flock over just feeding themselves (verse 3).

God expects us to give to others as we have received. It's ok to eat and wear clothes, but the primary goal is to prepare to feed others.

Teach others to feed for themselves, then they can go on to the scriptures when they need to. God is speaking to believers.

All our lives of training, preparing, studying is to train others to do it. So, learn to teach them and they will do it too. Believe in this godly principle.

Mature believers of scripture can change their ways by loving the flock, bringing them back to God, and refusing to be cruel to them (verse 4–5).

God is pointing out our shortcomings before his eyes on helping others. "The diseased have ye not strengthened," means God watches our neglect over the people. "Neither have ye sought that which was lost." God wants us all to be soul winners. "And they became meat to all the beasts of the field," The elements of nature were allowed to destroy God's people because of the neglect of them.

Our job is to help bring sick to healing, usefulness, growth, and then leadership or initiative. We all can do something with what we are given. Let's help others and get out of the self-help only mentality.

Mature believers of scripture can change their ways by helping the scattered ones return to God and his flock (verse 6).

We are to befriend the scattered people, so God will draw them back to the flock. The verse tells us that God's sheep were scattered through all the mountains. We should befriend people so that we can show them the way back to God from the waywardness they are at. "None did search or seek after them." We must use scripture to help them find their way back, as we used it for ourselves.

Let's gather scattered people and bring them back to the fold. We can share Jesus with them and feed and clothe them. The protection of God will sustain them all.

Chapter 7

The light of God's Word in the community we reside in

EACH PHASE OF LOVING OR NOT LOVING GOD'S WORD EFFECTS EACH OTHER AND SHOWS UP IN COMMUNITY. INCLUDING SUFFERING AND VILIFYING THE BELIEVER FOR NOT BEING ABLE TO TAKE THEIR STAND.

Our experiential knowledge of God always shows up in community leadership situations; therefore, guard from the lies against truth which are populated and taught. We must be ready and know how to stand up to the barrage of lies and attacks against our God and our faith.

Our experiential knowledge of God always shows up in community leadership situations; therefore, watch out how truth is constantly covered, removed, and made of non-effect. Be ready to note how the community of certain elitists will barrage your faith to remove, cover, and make it of non-effect.

Our experiential knowledge of God always shows up in community leadership situations; therefore, observe how community members are recipients of programmed agenda. Programmed agenda teaches or indoctrinates against traditional Christian values: to rebuke and destabilize the faith.

Our experiential knowledge of God always shows up in community leadership situations; therefore, be on guard for opposing beliefs which put out the fire and light of God's Word like: Socialism, Atheism, Gnosticism, Evolutionism, etc. The alternative secular humanistic ideas are the very system traditional Christianity has frowned upon.

Our experiential knowledge of God always shows up in community leadership situations; therefore, hold fast the position (be purified in the fire) for faith, belief, following Jesus Christ, reading scripture: all of which is discouraged and downplayed. We don't have to lose our faith, God, or beliefs: but we will go through the fire, and we can be triumphant in Jesus Christ.

<u>THE COMMUNITY WE RESIDE IN.</u>

Each phase of having or not having God's Word affects each other and shows up in community. Including suffering, vilifying the believer for past Christians not standing. If you're isolated and vilified, you can be sure that in your community there has been past animosity and jousting between Christians and others. Anyone, from this point on, must follow God's wisdom. Don't handle it yourself.

Line upon line will be the measure for success as you follow God's leading. As God reveals and the opponent ignores, God shall prove a prophet in the land. The Holy Spirit can handle it, can we, though? We will have to know doctrine on specific teachings and how we are to live. We will study in odd and trying times for our success in God. Work at it patiently because God will not fail us. Someone in our community will turn to God because of us. This is our experience, so cherish it. The Holy Spirit will be our authority and helper.

We will have to encourage ourselves often. Speaking in our inner dialogue and sanctifying God in it. Standing carefully without creating more trouble. We must pick our battles carefully and not rock the boat. Therefore, try not to violate others by our words, let our words be fitly spoken. Pray to God often.

We will need to often examine contextual settings to see whether something was done by us, others, or freak of nature: then address it appropriately. Love and speak truth with all people. Be a responsible adult in the community. Pray for its success, then we also will succeed.

<u>IN THE COMMUNITY: COMMUNITY WAYWARDNESS LEADS TO CONFUSION OF FACE.</u>

Within community, the way people hold truth is seen by God in all places; usually, people hold truth in error. Lies are populated, truth is meshed over, or removed. People now are being programmed. All the things happening within Society are stealing our light and fire, attempting to put out the heat, light, and flame. Nationally, there are movements to crush the influence and sacrifice from culture in life.

People have enjoyed a life of leisure for so long that either service to God or a life of submission to him seems ridiculous. Because the community has hardened down on the godly order and common sense, the Word is cast to the wind. People like the American dream or good life as opposed to biblical precedence. They would rather fill their dreams instead of God's dreams for them.

Our admonition is to seek first the Kingdom of God, then all these things will be added. Denying ourselves, taking up our cross and following Jesus Christ is the biblical precedence. Seeking to obey God with our gifts, talents, and abilities helps the community to be a blessing. Being faithful using theology helps us live out the Word. Let's carry out our stewardship for the community; seek and pray for its safety and success, so we also will be blessed through it.

<u>IN COMMUNITY, WE MUST TAKE TO HEART
THAT OUR CONTINUED WAYWARDNESS LEADS
US TO CONFUSION OF FACE.</u>

And at the evening sacrifice I arose up from my heaviness; and having rent my garment and my mantle, I fell upon my knees, and spread out my hands unto the LORD my God, and said, O my God, I am ashamed and blush to lift up my face to thee, my God: for our iniquities are increased over *our* head, and our trespass is grown up unto the heavens. Since the days of our fathers *have,* we *been* in a great trespass unto this day; and for our iniquities have we, our kings, *and* our priests, been delivered into the hand of the kings of the lands, to the sword, to captivity, and to a spoil, and to confusion of face, as *it is* this day. And now for a little space grace hath been *shewed* from the LORD our God, to leave us a remnant to escape, and to give us a nail in his holy place, that our God may lighten our eyes, and give us a little reviving in our bondage. For we *were* bondmen; yet our God hath not forsaken us in our bondage, but hath extended mercy unto us in the sight of the kings of Persia, to give us a reviving, to set up the house of our God, and to repair the desolations thereof, and to give us a wall in Judah and in Jerusalem. And now, O our God, what shall we say after this? For we have forsaken thy commandments, which thou hast commanded by thy servants the prophets, saying, the land, unto which ye go to possess it, is an unclean land with the filthiness of the people of the lands, with their abominations, which have filled it from one end to another with their uncleanness. Now therefore give not your daughters unto their sons, neither take their daughters unto your sons, nor seek their peace or their wealth forever: that ye may be strong, and eat the good of the land, and leave *it* for an inheritance to your children forever. And after all that is come upon us for our evil deeds, and for our great trespass, seeing that thou our God hast punished us less than our iniquities *deserve*, and hast given us *such* deliverance as this; should we again break thy commandments, and join in affinity with the people of these abominations? Wouldest not thou be angry with us till thou hadst consumed *us*, so that *there should be* no remnant nor escaping? O LORD God of Israel, thou *art* righteous: for we remain yet escaped, as *it is* this day: behold, we *are* before thee in our trespasses: for we cannot stand before thee because of this. **Ezra 9:5–15 (KJV)**

Continued waywardness leads to confusion of face because great trespass leads a people to captivity (verses 5-7).

As a community, we must seek God often, so God can purge us from our lack of consecration to him. We should come to God in our burden, shame, confessing our sin, and expressing how our shame of face is because of sin. The verse speaks of a heaviness. It's our weight of sin which we must seek God for relief. "Confusion of face," is disgrace and shame within community, therefore seek God.

It's open community sin and shame which when acknowledged, confessed, and repented upon turning to Jesus brings satisfaction.

If we don't live from the bible then we allow ourselves to plunge head first into the cauldron of sin, thus, we will fail. God has to be made the center of our life. He, alone, can keep us from sin's pull.

Continued waywardness leads to confusion of face because when continued it cuts people off from God's help through commandment breaking.

Waywardness or turning away from what is right and proper will be judged. God will not tolerate uncontested abandonment of his ways. The verse says, "A little reviving in our bondage." Which means upon great trespass comes various forms of bondage. God wants to revive any people who will turn to him. But the scriptures go on to say, "We have forsaken our commandments." But what can we do when the people who were revived again break God's commands? Whole nations and their communities, maybe cut right off because of sin.

Obedience starts with the character of individuals and spreads to groups. If we allow God and his Word to have first place, we will find the trail of life. It appears it is lost, but the path of life is still there, perhaps we haven't walked on it lately.

Continued waywardness leads to confusion of face because it strips a community of her strength (11-12).

A sinning people without God's influence is a land destined for desolation. Our life should be lived for God over and above success, wealth, goods, etc. Put God first and then those will be added. The verse speaks of the, "Filthiness of the people of the land." The land cries out because of its inhabitant's sins before God. God is calling people of any nationality to repent and be healed.

We all have the opportunity to seek and walk with God. This is our call so that God is pleased in blessing our land and posterity. God seeks a godly seed for us.

Continued waywardness leads to confusion of face because when a people join with the unrighteous (God-haters);

the godly people cannot stand (verses 13-15).

When the sin of a community becomes full and is judged, seeing the evil befall the nation, should the people again strive with God through breaking his Word? This is the way a people fall and cannot stand. "God has punished us less than our iniquities deserve." God's graciously gives us a chance to show we repent, love God, and will walk with him. But our line is shallow, soon, "we are before thee in our trespasses: for we cannot stand before thee because of this." When we add sin upon sin, it equals in-ability before God.

Repent community to the gospel in the bible and trust Jesus Christ personally with a personal change in our beliefs, actions, and our pursuit of God.

Chapter 8

General Problems

USUALLY, WE FEEL LITTLE DESIRE FOR THE INFLUENCE OF THE WORD OF GOD, AND THEREFORE, NO STUDY AND NO PREPARATION FOR LEARNING SCRIPTURE OCCURS. PEOPLE REFUSE OR DON'T KNOW HOW TO STUDY.

It is my desire to motivate all who read this book to set ourselves to grow through bible reading and training. Going back to bible development.

If we don't study bible scripture, our light goes out in all areas. I wonder how you feel when your light goes out? To me, it feels like the nastiest and most evil thing. Keep God's Will in your life through scripture reading and study, that is our light.

If we don't study ignorance goes on with its consequences. When we lead our lives in ignorance, even if we have a morality and experience; we are led to the slaughter because we prove useless.

If we don't study people will judge us by mere opinion with no help from God to instruct us. Our study must acquire bible meaning, contextual settings as it applies today, and application: buy a book that teaches you this: How to study scripture.

If we don't learn, read, and interpret scripture, then we will read our own ideas into the Word of God. There is danger in that. Where we read our ideas, it is opposed to how God wants us to understand. We instruct ourselves wrong instead of acquiring the proper meaning of the passage. If you haven't learned to interpret; then use a dictionary to look up the meaning of the words and understand it that way.

If we don't read and study, we choose opinion for meaning. I can assure you, talk to people in Church, many go by opinion instead of direct biblical inspiration.

If we don't study, we won't have God's prerogative, and we will fail to observe his Will at all times. Our reading and prayer should open us to God's Will and ways for our life.

<u>GENERAL PROBLEMS ADDRESSED.</u>

Sadly, Christians usually feel little desire or drive for the influence of studying the Word of God; therefore, no study and preparation gets done. People simply don't know any study methods. Be sure, if it's been days or more, the influence may go out. You need a study method. I'll say from the onset-there are good books you can buy on, "How to study the bible." Get one. If anything, read scripture with a dictionary.

Get in the bible to avoid all the general problems associated with half-hazard reading. Scripture speaks of the key of knowledge. This could be yours if you learn to unlock scripture truth and apply it in your struggle. Don't read your ideas into the text, instead hear what it's saying and apply it. Be sure to follow sound doctrine and study daily to acquire the training techniques you need to learn. As you study, you will progress. You'll grow in experienced knowledge of God and his Will. God will speak to you about what his will is for you. The truth will come alive for you.

LITTLE DESIRE FOR THE INFLUENCE OF GOD'S WORD, NO STUDY OR PREPARATIONS FOR LEARNING SCRIPTURE; THIS BECOMES THE NORMAL CHRISTIAN'S PROBLEM.

Because there is no effort to read and study scripture, the light of God's Word goes out. Ignorance goes on and it bears negative consequences. Opinions ruin the real fruit of God's Word. All these things cause failure in the larger community setting and common community places like cities, jobs, families, etc.

<u>WE CAN AVOID BEING A BAD EXAMPLE TO OTHERS.</u>

If thou put the brethren in remembrance of these things, thou shalt be a good minister of Jesus Christ, nourished up in the words of faith and of good doctrine, whereunto thou hast attained. But refuse profane and old wives' fables, and exercise thyself rather unto godliness. For bodily exercise profiteth little: but godliness is profitable unto all things, having promise of the life that now is, and of that which is to come. This is a faithful saying and worthy of all acceptation. For therefore we both labor and suffer reproach because we trust in the living God, who is the Savior of all men, specially of those that believe. These things command and teach. Let no man despise thy youth; but be thou an example of the believers, in word, in conversation, in charity, in spirit, in faith, in purity. Till I come, give attendance to reading, to exhortation, to doctrine. Neglect not the gift that is in thee, which was given thee by prophecy, with the laying on of the hands of the presbytery. Meditate upon these things; give thyself wholly to them; that thy profiting may appear to all. Take heed unto thyself, and unto the doctrine; continue in them: for in doing this thou shalt both save thyself, and them that hear thee. 1 Timothy 4:6-16 (KJV)

We can avoid being a bad example to others by putting others in remembrance of the godly things attained (verse 6).

Our objective in walking in biblical influence is to allow God's influence to help us put things in perspective on what God has done by way of remembrance.

"Put the brethren in remembrance." Don't prove people wrong, but show them what the Word of God says and what God has done. We want the people, "nourished up in the Words of faith." God has allowed certain attainment for people who were nourished in Words of faith. This is the goal. All good is from God, and we live in all the goodness that God has provided.

Remember and remind others of what God has done. Let God lift your heart and make himself real to you. This will solidify God's Will for you.

We can avoid being a bad example to others by excluding fleshly ideas and including godly ways (verses 7-8).

We can avoid being bad examples by using scripture to set aside fleshly ways and incorporating God's ways. Get the fake love out and get godliness in.

Practice God's presence and Word for eternal benefits. "Refuse old wives fables." There are things we say no to, and on the other hand, we practice godliness. The verse alludes to bodily exercises. The things of one's body are important; but not anything like God's eternal will and mindset we should have. We must acquire a mind which puts all things into perspective with God having priority, then the rest.

The bible read, studied, obeyed gives us practical insight as to God's will for our life. We must acquire this to be a lamp on a hill. From time-to-time, God will allow us to grab and pull in lost souls.

We can avoid being a bad example to others by laboring and suffering reproach for those who believe (verses 9-11).

We live in a world where we no longer stand with those who suffer for Jesus. It seems to be the believers who initiate a contention with fellow believers they feel are radical. "We labor and suffer reproach in the verse means that it is our dual call to labor and suffer. This is because we trust in God. We suffer because we belong to God.

We are commanded to teach these things, and this will warn the righteous Christ is coming.

We can avoid being a bad example to others by modeling a Christlike life (verses 12-13).

The bible exhorts us to model a Christlike life before all people. Wherever we find ourselves, we should walk with God in and through it. Be Christlike before all. We should not let any man despise our youth-the verse tells us. We don't have to shy away from anyone who tries to control us, especially if you have greater bible knowledge and a real walk with God. In your conversation, be like Jesus before all. Attend to bible reading and exhortation. Learn bible doctrine.

We can avoid being a bad example to others by stirring up our gift and staying in sound doctrine (verses 14–16).

We have a gift, and we are to stir it up and use it. Stay in scripture admonition and its practical advice for life. "Neglect not the gift within thee." We should work our gift and use it for the promotion of the good news. Meditate on scripture to use it in life settings.

We convince the naysayers by our good conduct and gifting. Let us be strong through study, etc.

Chapter 9
The Supernatural battle

I will attempt to paint a picture for you how God has our interest at heart. Satan, will pave a way for people, but knows who-ever follows him suffers the same fate as he. We are given choice, responsibility, and accountability.

1. What we believe-choice.
2. How we live our life-responsibility.
3. One day, we will account for the choices, actions, and our attitude toward God.

This is important to know in Spiritual warfare. Our choices, responsibilities, and accountabilities are essential in Spiritual warfare.

Choices, responsibilities, and accountability are important in spiritual warfare because the enemy will use strategy against you. Choices and responsibility help you choose your values that define you and enable you to hold your position within the community.

Choices, responsibilities, and accountability are important in spiritual warfare because the enemy will paint a picture. Accountability is essential, as Satan tries to visualize for you a different you then what God gave you to be accountable to him for.

Choices, responsibilities, and accountability are important in spiritual warfare because the enemy will play on your personality. Be responsible to your position and your required obedience before God, and God will enable you to keep your identity in Jesus.

Choices, responsibilities, and accountability are important in spiritual warfare because the enemy will lead you astray. Satan is always seeking to steal the

Word away, so we cannot be what God says-don't let him.

<u>SPIRITUAL WARFARE ADDRESSED.</u>

I want you to know that if you choose to read the bible and be a lifelong applier of God' Word: Satan is going to fight you. No greater thing is there to expose Satan then God's Word. Crazy and mysterious things will happen to you. You have to get vigilant, diligent, and continue as you apply God's Word: Satan will try to steal all of it.

The bible goal is to bare godly fruit and be faithful as a steward over God's Word in your life: This is where your battle will be. This is where particular doctrines and the Holy Spirit's leading plays a major part in your daily living. Having knowledge of basic or fundamental Christianity will be essential. Bill Bright's book, "A handbook for Christian Maturity," is a good source to learn Christian basics.

Moving forward and having vision becomes essential to move out of one's battle to grazing ground once again- until the next battle. I will not lie; studying scripture is basic training for spiritual warfare: trusting God from one battle to the next. Key:

1. You gain when you win, things to lay at the Master's feet.

2. You grow stronger as you trust God through the struggles, and battles: if you blow up, you can say goodbye to your victory- Satan will run away with it.

<u>WHAT THE SUPERNATURAL BATTLE REVEALS: THE TEST OF COMBAT DETERMINES ONE'S SPIRITUAL FOUNDATION'S WORTHINESS.</u>

But Abner the son of Ner, captain of Saul's host, took Ishbosheth the son of Saul, and brought him over to

Mahanaim; and made him king over Gilead, and over the Ashurites, and over Jezreel, and over Ephraim, and over Benjamin, and over all Israel. Ishbosheth Saul's son was forty years old when he began to reign over Israel, and reigned two years. But the house of Judah followed David. And the time that David was king in Hebron over the house of Judah was seven years and six months. And Abner the son of Ner, and the servants of Ishbosheth the son of Saul, went out from Mahanaim to Gibeon. And Joab the son of Zeruiah, and the servants of David, went out, and met together by the pool of Gibeon: and they sat down, the one on the one side of the pool, and the other on the other side of the pool. And Abner said to Joab, Let the young men now arise, and play before us. And Joab said, let them arise. Then there arose and went over by number twelve of Benjamin, which pertained to

Ishbosheth the son of Saul, and twelve of the servants of David. And they caught everyone his fellow by the head, and thrust his sword in his fellow's side; so, they fell down together: wherefore that place was called Helkathhazzurim, which is in Gibeon. And there was a very sore battle that day; and Abner was beaten, and the men of Israel, before the servants of David. 2 Samuel 2:8-17 (KJV)

1. Combat will try a spiritual foundation's worthiness by challenging the loyalty one has to the authority one trusts in (Verses 8-9).
2. Combat will try a spiritual foundation's worthiness by always presenting different or differing viewpoints or world views (Verses 10-11).
3. Combat will try a spiritual foundation's worthiness by

bringing a person or group directly before an opposing force (Verses 12-13).

4. Combat will try a spiritual foundation's worthiness by determining each person's combat readiness and one's loyalty to God, their leader, and their community (verses 14-15).

5. Combat will try a spiritual foundation's worthiness by causing all too either die, quit, or press on in Jesus Christ (verses 16-17).

EXERCISING STRATEGIC SPIRITUAL WARFARE: IF WE WILL KEEP GOD'S LIGHT BURNING INSIDE US-PLANNING, FIGHTING, PREPARING, AND CHANGING THE SITUATION TO ACHIEVE A GOOD ATMOSPHERE FOR STUDY IS A MUST ON OUR BEHALF.

Gather your books: remember we need skillful friends in God's Word, to encourage us to face abuses against God's Word. We must be willing to be trained spiritually by the bible. Experience tells us we face violence against us for bible training. We must train our children. The Word will equip our people for what is needed. We not only prepare, but maintain God's order. Obtain resources and be responsible with them and account to God for them. Pleasing God is a sacrifice that cost's us something because it comes from true love and from following Jesus Christ.

We are confronted with the awful contest to wage war for the right to use scripture in all areas of our life. There are people, demons, and a lot of other things competing for loyalty of our time. Do you purpose to undertake the combat? Probably, of all the attacks which Satan is levying against us, today; He most likely uses all to keep us from knowing God, all the other attacks serve this end. If we will not or cannot get into the

Holy Bible, Satan will attempt to take us captive.

And that they may recover themselves out of the snare of the devil, who are taken captive by him at his will. 2 Timothy 2:26 (KJV)

We must war in the power of the finished work of Calvary and the anointing of the Holy Spirit. We can mobilize or make ready to war by stirring our hearts up afresh for God's Word, and keeping our sights on intensity for God's cause in our life. Realize to keep this most precious of gifts in our life (the Word of God), and a clean conscience; we will fight for it. Basically, we fight for this liberty through abnormal ways of a wayward society.

First consecrate yourself to God by praying, doing his Will, and asking his help, etc. Face off with your enemy on God's terms. Proceed with your preparations as necessary. We have an unseen enemy who puts God's people in derision as often as possible. If we do not stand up to this wicked force, then our way of life will be eradicated for what I call stupid pettiness and nothingness. This battle in the spiritual domain shows who are alive in their position, who is programmed, who the cannon-fodder of the elitists are, etc. We have to know our bible and hold fast our position. Your plan of action must include when to take your stand for God's Word and not to. You must know your objective for study.

Upon your daily personal study and prayer, be ready for battles within the war. Continue to seek God through the battles, and do not assume you won't have them. Determine how you're going to fight and prepare that way. Follow the Holy Spirit's leading through each battle. We are at war with the world over the right to live out our way of life. Not a physical war, but a war of the mind. We are at war with the flesh, and the devil over our right to read, comment on, and live out the biblical principles. We must engage in battle when our interests to read and live out biblical mandates are at stake. Stand in the gap. Suffering is not always avoidable; we have to enforce religious liberty in all types of situations. Set goals, pray for God's guidance, assemble your network, and establish foundation and acquire ground won. Choose and hold positions and attitudes necessary for the win, and keep the ground won.

Remember to pick your battles carefully. After war, draw down to peace with neighbors again. We are commanded to love one another and be at peace if at all possible. We have to return to providing and earning our pay and to serve our God given purpose as our God given mission to serve others. Review why the battle happened and what you are to retain from it. Set in motion what was accomplished in it.

Conclusion to Keep the Fire of God's Word Burning in your Heart

We as citizens of the great Nation of the United States of America stand at a cross road; which we have stood here for some time now. The majority of the population has taken the broad road to the American Dream. I do believe in the American Dream; but not at the expense of throwing out God and the biblical way of life. We can have success with God as head and scripture as the authoritative rule in our lives.

We need to keep our Christian heritage at all costs because there is no other nation that can or will come in and restore to us our Christian roots. Once it (our national roots in God) is gone; the people have spoken out against their God; and God will turn us over to our own devices. The nation that forgets its God shall be turned into hell.

Let's not be afraid to read and comment on the bible; and share the truths within it. Observe that people have died to bring us our copy of the scriptures, and we should hold the scriptures up as our light in life.

9 781964 037233